YOGIRAJ SWAMI NANDLAL JI MAHARAJ - A BIOGRAPHY

ANEESH TRAKROO

Made with ♥ on the Notion Press Platform
www.notionpress.com

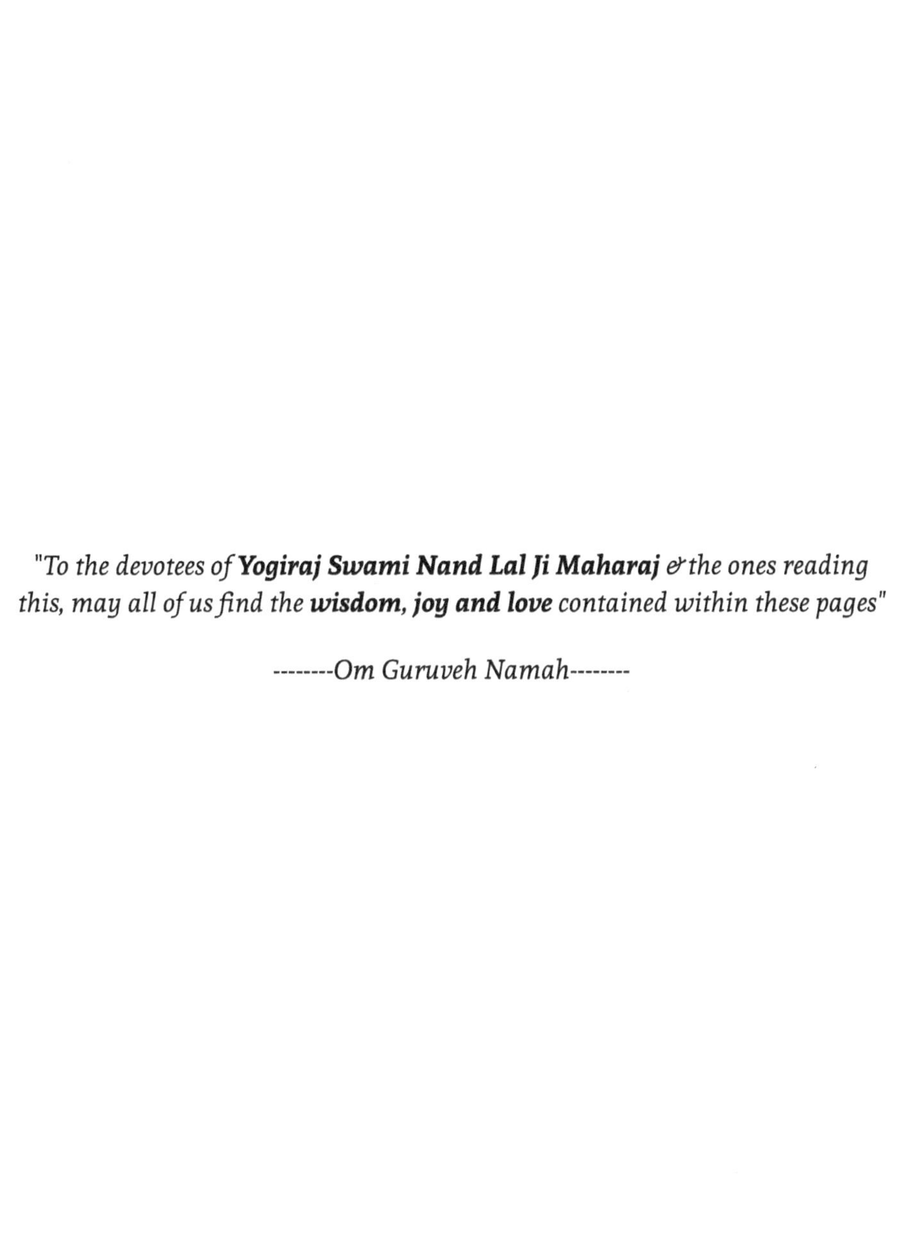
"To the devotees of **Yogiraj Swami Nand Lal Ji Maharaj** & the ones reading this, may all of us find the **wisdom, joy and love** contained within these pages"

--------Om Guruveh Namah--------

Contents

Foreword

Its Ethereal... Thought-Provoking... & Full of Spritual Wisdom !
I hope this book reaches the right people... !
*& May **Guru Maharaj** blesses all of us with all the happiness in the world !*

Anuvrat Tikkoo (Swami Ji's Devotee)
Journalist & Editor, New York

Preface

The Author declares that he will only share the truth & nothing else only after checking all the resources & references available...!

Acknowledgements

The author would like to acknowledge the help of all the people involved in this project and, more specifically, to the editors and reviewers that took part in the review process. Without their support, this book would not have become a reality.

First, the author would like to thank each one of the editors for their contributions. Our sincere gratitude goes to the chapter's editors who contributed their time and expertise to this book.

Second, the authors wish to acknowledge the valuable contributions of the reviewers regarding the improvement of quality, coherence, and content presentation of chapters. Most of the editors also served as referees; we highly appreciate their double task.

First Editor's Name
Subramanium Sundaram, Tamil Nadu

Second Editor's Name
Preeji Nair, Gurgaon

Prologue

Once upon a time in the Northernmost part of India, Kashmir.... a young boy lived ! Although he had everything, his heart desired, yet he was confused about...

But then one winter's night, an old beggar woman came to his house and offered him a single rose in return for shelter from the bitter cold...

Repulsed by her haggard appearance, the boy sneered at the gift and turned the old woman away. But she warned him not to be deceived by appearances, for beauty is found within, the soul.....

And when he dismissed her again, the old woman's ugliness melted away to reveal a beautiful enchantress...

ONE
THE BLESSED CHILD

Agnyaan Ghatey Sirye Prakaash Chukh Aasewonuy
Gyane Prakaash Chukh Aasewonuy
Hee Myane Satguru Kshene Kshene Chum Aasare Chonuy
-Pt. Neelkanth Ji

This is the story of a **mystic saint, a superhuman, a perfect yogi, a spritual master** who still resides in the hearts of all his devotees. This is the story of **Yogiraj Paramguru Swami Nand Lal Ji Maharaj !...**

So, let us start from the start...

Swami Nand Lal Ji was born in the year **1902** in the **Gurgari Mohalla, Zaina Kadal, Srinagar.** He was born in a prosperous family, who were also known as **"Kothdars"** that time. His grandfather **Pandit Sehza Kaul** had two sons **Ram Kaul** and **Hara Kaul.** Swami Ji was the son of **Pandit Hara Kaul.** Swami Ji was born on an auspicious day, **Falgun Shukla Paksh Ashtami (Taila Ashtami).** Swami Ji's fore-fathers were prominent bankers. It is said, they were bankers even to **Maharaja Pratap Singh.** They were ardent devotees of **Goddess Jagadamba Sharika Devi.** Be it the pleasant summer or cold winter, both males and females in the family would go for **Parikrama** to the Holy Mother at **Hari-Parbat. Swami Nand Lal Ji's** mother died very young, leaving behind her two sons and one daughter and that was the beginning of **Swami Ji** journey towards the goal which he had left halfway in his previous **Janama.**

SWAMI NAND LAL JI MAHARAJ

It is said that his childhood at his home was not comfortable as his mother had passed away when he was quite young so he left his home at the **age 14** while he was in **Class 9**[th] only. His step-mother was his first Guru whose way of life had a great influence on **Swami Ji**. In fact, he was not destined to be an ordinary householder, he was here for a larger mission. His birth was a blessing for many of us & many to come.

<u>Young Swami Nand Lal Ji</u>

Thus **Swami Ji** detached himself at an early age from the bondages of the household life to seek a higher purpose for himself. In search of the ultimate path, **Young Swami Ji** remained on move from place to place, from one saint to another till one day around **1932-33,** he reached **Zooni-Pora, Bomai Ashram (Kupwara)** where he found his guru **Swami Lal Ji Maharaj.**

Rare Photograph of Swami Nand Lal Ji

Swami Nand Lal Ji was very energetic in his youth and would command his fellow companions. **Swami Ji** was very kind at heart and full of love and compassion. Swami Nand Lal Ji studied up to **8**th **class** & when he became a **Yogi**, many of his friends turned into his ardent devotees. **Swami Ji** also started some sort of business for a short period of time. At the age of **17 or 18 years**, Swami Ji left for his **Sadhana** . Once he left his parental house, he never looked back. **Young Swami Ji** was unraceable for a long period of almost**twenty years.**

TWO

SWAMI LAL JI OF BANARAS - THE SOURCE

Param Poojaniya Swami Lal Ji Maharaj was a **perfect yogi**, expert in **Sanskrit Para Vidya** and **Sri Vidya**. He was the **Head Mahant** of **Sri Chaitanya Gaudia Math, Banaras.** Swami Lal Ji had experience of **Shakti Padh** for **30 years.** Swami Lal Ji was the brother disciple of **Sri Shiv Rattan Gir** who also was a great saint, who also built the Ashram & famous **Durga Nag Temple** in **Srinagar. Durga Nag** is one of the oldest religious places of Kashmiri Hindus, which because of its spiritual sanctity has been attracting saints of highest order from time to time who would stay at this place for their elevation to the highest spiritual order.

Swami Lal Ji Maharaj

Zooni-PoraAshram ofBomai,Kupwara - This Ashram was destined to be the ultimate destination for young **Nand Lal Ji** to get associated with lots of saints and sadhus. This was the only place where he met his spritual guru **Swami Lal Ji,** a highly accomplished yogi. The Ashram used to be full of known saints & fakirs all the time because it came on the way to **Maa Sharda Temple, Titwal (Gurez)** that is now in **Muzzafarabad, Pakistan Occupied Kashmir**. The devotees on the way to **Sharda Temple,** used to stay in **Zooni-Pora Ashram, Bomai** for a couple of days or more for the facilities available and seek blessings of **Mata.**

Sharda Peeth, P.O.K (Today)

Swami Lal Ji, though being a **Non-Kashmiri** saint, was frequently paying his obeisance at **Durga Nag Temple, Shankaracharya Temple, Chakrishour** in **Tulmul** and essentially at **Mata Sharda Temple** which is now in **POK**. He would often visit **Kashmir Valley** in the **September** month & spend some days there to seek blessings of Sharda Mata. It is said that in **1947 (Sep-Oct)**, when **Pakistan** was planning an attack on **Kashmir,Swami Lal Ji** was there at the **Maa Sharda Temple** & left just a few days before terrorists attacked the temple. Swami lal ji left for Banaras in october 1947 & post one year in 1948 he took **Maha Samadhi** in his **Banaras Ashram.**

<u>Sri Chaitanya Gaudiya Math, Banaras</u> (1939)

THREE
GURU, SADHANA & PLACES

The **Zooni-Pora Ashram** in those days **(1932-40)** was headed by **Pandit Shiv Jee Shah** who managed all the affairs of the **Ashram** along with a huge property attached to it. A regular **LANGAR** was arranged to cater hundreds of visitors daily. All the food-grains, vegetables and fruits consumed in the ashram were the product of the farmland attached to it tended by the farmers nearby.

<u>Statue of Swami Lal Ji & Swami Nand Lal Ji Maharaj</u>

Before **Swami Ji** was initiated into the ascetic order by his holiness **Swami Lal Ji**, he had a long stay in the **Zooni-Pora Ashram** in the service of numerous saints present there. By keeping attendance of many learned souls he adhered to the high disciplined saintly life. Thus **Swami Ji** received the choicest education of saint order. Their learnings included the study of various religious scriptures and especially the practice of Yoga. Thus **Zooni-Pora Ashram** proved to be the basic school of learning for **Swami Ji** and also a place where he had the occasion to be in the feet of his Guru.

Swami Lal Ji (Guru) was so much impressed with **Swami Nand Lal Ji's** (Shishya)sadhna, that at one point of time, he offered his **Aasana** to **Swami Ji. Swami Ji** humbly refused to accept the offer as it is not right in the **Guru-Shishya** relationship. **Swami Lal Ji** took so many years to master a kriya but the same was done by his shishya, **Swami Ji** in a very short period of time. **Swami Ji's** way of life and **Sadhana**, left a lot of impact on his **Guru Maharaj. Swami Nand Lal Ji** gained a lot of spritual mastery in his youth alone.

While **Swami Ji** was in **Zooni-Pora Ashram** being probably the youngest, he was occasionally sent for some petty errands to village **Bomai** just a kilometer away, which comprised of a good number of (**around 60-70**)

Pandit families.

Sh. Jia Lal Dass, a reputed person of village **Bomai** was especially attached to young **Swami Ji** for his attractive yogic appearance and cheerful aspect. One day **Swami Ji** expressed his desire to **Pandit Dass** to stay in his house & pursue Sadhna there. **Sh. Jia Lal Ji** talked about it in his family and **Smt Radha Mali**, his mother, a saintly lady immediately consented to it and with full devotion and sanctity offered everything whatever **Swami Ji** needed to pursue his sadhna there. Thus **Swami Ji** was offered to stay in **Deewan-Khan** which was the first floor of a wooden structure just opposite Pandit Dass's House. Swami Ji wanted a seperate space for his sadhana with a seperate entry. It was quite a large joint family of about fifty members and everyone was excited to have **Swami Ji** in their house. So they extended all possible services to **Swami Ji.** Their service and devotion with all sanctity to Swami Ji and his numberless visitors at all odd hours for years together is unparalleled. **Swami Ji** stayed in this **Deewan-Khan** for about **8-10 years** before he shifted to a **Kutiya** in **Gowri-Pora, Bomai.**

<u>Swami Lal Ji Maharaj</u>

The period of Swami Ji's stay in **Zooni-Pora Ashram** and later in the **Deewan-Khan** was the formative period of his holy life. He almost all the time, remained absorbed in **Yog-Kriya** besides being on the move meeting **Saints and Sadhus** &visiting various places of religious importance. His way of doing sadhana & his yogic journey was very different from other yogis. It has been reported that he used to visit remote interiors of unknown dense forests and stay there for long periods with other highly awakened souls.

Also, all these years, **Swami Ji** was a regular visitor to **Sharda-Mata Temple,** now in **P.O.K.** The visits there involved a long travel on foot and later on horses through **Kupwara** and **Lolab Valley.** While travelling, he along with his associates used to stay in the houses of some **Kashmiri Pandits** of that area. This association created a vast field of devotees and admirers of **Swami Ji** in that area. This is the time when one of the greatest events in Swami Ji's life, happened. This is where the formal initiation of **Swami Ji** to saintly ordertook place by his Guru & Holiness "**Swami Lal Ji Maharaj**".

<u>Swami Nand Lal Jiwith his devotees</u>

Since **Swami Lal Ji** also used to visit **Sharda Temple** regularly & stayed with **Pandits** there. He too had a large number of devotees in that area & On the occasion of **Swami Ji's** formal initiation to saintly order, **Swami Lal Ji** (His Guru) himself looked for a place for him to perform the initiation kriya in **Sogam village, Kopwara.** The popularity of **Swami Ji** spread far and wide while he settled at the **Deewan-Khan** in **Bomai.** His thirst for knowledge was so great that he had mastered almost all ancient **scriptures**, a highly regarded scholar and teacher, he was.

After spending so manyyears in **Deewan-Khan** with **Dass family** in **Bomai** village, **Swami Ji** thought of changing his place of sadhna. And this time **Swami Ji** selected a beautiful lush green spot near **Gowri-Pora village** & constructed a **Kutiya** in an apple orchard which also belonged to the same **Dass family.** This place was about a kilometer away from **Bomai.** In due course a small **Ashram** with a couple of rooms & kitchen was raised there under the directions of **Swami Ji.** All essentials were provided to **Swami Ji.** The compound was walled with dry willow twigs and a small entry gate was provided to keep stray animals and cattle away from the compound.

As the field of devotees expanded with time, there was a need for more ashrams in the name of **Swami Ji.** Eventually, two Ashrams, one at **Tikkar (Kupwara)** and the other at **Hushoora village** in **Budgam District** came up. Both the **Ashrams** were planned by **Swami Ji** himself. The venues of the **Ashrams** were also selected by **Swami Ji.** Specially, the **Tikkar (Kupwara) Ashram** was tastefully planned by **Swami Ji** since he preferred staying in that **Ashram** than in any other Ashram. He actually stayed there for longer periods, in his later life also. The **Hushoora Ashram** was constructed before **Tikkar Ashram** and was raised on the request of **Swami Ji's** devotees of that area. **Swami Ji** stayed there for many days and performed many **Hawans** as well. Devotees there always showed great enthusiasm and devotion for **Swami Ji.** This **Ashram** always used to remain full of devotees. **Swami Ji's** selection of places and his architectural tastes were superb.

YOGIRAJ SU SHREE SWAMI NAND LAL JI & BHAKTHJAN BIRLA MANDIR DELHI

FOUR
LAL-DED & SWAMI JI

In **Sopore,** a galaxy of saints and learned Pandits used to occasionally meet in a temple for discussions and discourses regarding Hindu scriptures. **Swami Ji** and his **Guru Swami Lal Ji** also use to be a part of those discussions. It is said that **Swami Ji** used to show a lot of interest in the interpretations of famous **"VakhsofLal-Ded".** He would usually refer the **"Vakhs of Lalleshwari" (Lalla-Vakhs)** in his **discourses** as an authentic treatise and explain it to everyone with lot of passion.

    Who wasLal-Ded ?

Lal-Ded (Lalleshwari)

Lal-Ded was a rebel saint, a revolutionary mystic of the **14th century Kashmir**. We know her only through her verses called '**Vak**'; that have come down to us through folk tradition of Kashmir. Also known as **Lalla** or **Laleshwari, Lal Ded** was an ardent devotee of **God Shiva**. She also often used her poetry to engage with **Shaivism** and **Sufism**. **Lal Ded's** verses have come down from generations to generations through the folk tradition of **Kashmir** and perhaps there isn't a single Kashmiri who hasn't heard of her. **Lalleshwari** was known to be Kashmir's rebel poetess for she challenged the ideas of caste system, social and religious discrimination and rejected conventional society.

Lal-Ded, Born sometime around **1320 to 1355** in **Pandrethan** in a Kashmiri Pandit family. Later on, she came to be known by many names including **Lalla Arifa, Lalla Yogishwari, Lalla Yogini, Laleshwari** orsimply **Lalla**. After being briefly educated in the religious texts, she was married off at the age of **12** into a family that regularly mistreated her.

After being briefly educated in the religious texts, she was married off at the **age of 12** into a family that regularly mistreated her. Her mother-in-law treated her cruelly and spoke ill of her to her husband. Lalla's mother-in-law is known to have put stones on her plate of food and then covered it with rice. Even when she was not given proper food and always remained half-fed, **Lalleshwari** is known to never have complained.

Every morning, **Lal-Ded** left the house to fill a pot of water from the river and wouldn't return until it was evening; in-between, she spent her time at **Lord Shiva's** temple on the other side of the river.

Soon, she found her guru in **Sidh Srikanth** and pursued yoga under him. And when she turned around **26**, **Lalla** renounced her marriage and material life to become a **mystic**. Having given up all her possessions, she would wander around naked or in rags, chanting her verses.

Lal Ded's openness and her understanding of the genuine problems of the common people is what made her so immensely popular among millions. Even today, almost every Kashmiri, irrespective of whether he is **Hindu or Muslim**, literate or illiterate, is able to recite some of Lal Ded's Vakhs. Her name in the valley is said with utmost pride, admiration and respect. Her poetry has also been widely translated including English translations in **'Women in Praise of the Sacred: 43 Centuries of Spiritual Poetry by Women (1994)'**, **'Naked Song- Lalla (1992)'** and a lot more.

After having lived most of her life as a mystic and inspiring others, **Lal-Ded** took mahasamadi sometime during the late **14ᵗʰ century**.

All in all, **Lal-Ded** was a wise woman and a **genius poetess** with an un-shattering faith and confidence made her leave a mark on the world. By knowing more about her, there is no doubt that her contribution to Kashmiri language, culture, tradition as well as heritage is truly commendable. In fact, it is also often said- **'Lalla is to Kashmiri** what **Shakespeare is to English'**.

Some famous "**Lal-Vakhs**" translated in **English** :

I have seen an educated man starve,
a leaf blown off by bitter wind.
Once I saw a thoughtless fool beat his cook.
Lalla has been waiting for the allure of the world to fall away.
I might scatter the southern clouds, drain the sea, or cure someone hopelessly
ill.
But to change the mind of a fool is beyond me.
I came by the public road but won't return on it.
On the embankment I stand, halfway through the journey.
Day is gone. Night has fallen.
I dig in my pockets but can't find a cowry shell.
What can I pay for the ferry?
I, Lalla, entered the gate of the mind's garden and saw Siva united with
Sakti.
I was immersed in the lake of undying bliss. Here, in this lifetime, I've been
unchained from the wheel of birth and death.
What can the world do to me?
My guru gave a single precept: turn your gaze from outside to inside fix it on
the hidden self.
I, Lalla, took this to heart and naked set forth to dance

FIVE

THE FAMOUS KABALI RAID STORY

Undoubtedly, he excelled in the field of **Yoga** far above most of other **Kashmir Saints**. Very few saints of **Kashmir** including the highly awakened ones practiced **Yoga. Swami Ji** achieved the highest stages of self-realization through **Yoga** under the guidance of his Guru **"Swami Lal Ji"**.

He has won the title **Yogiraj** for his extraordinary capabilities he acquired in the field of **Yoga**.

<u>Swami Nand Lal Ji in Dhyaan</u>

Swami Ji was very much fond of nature and this had influenced his way of life. He was a total **vegetarian** and was fond of **sufiana music.** All singers of repute in this style of music would come and enthrall him by their ragas. After completion of his **Sadhana, Swami Ji** settled in the **Tanghdar** area of **Kashmir,** where he had a small **Ashram** in the famous shrine of **SharadaMata Temple.**

It was in the year **1947** when **Pakistanis** occupied that place & **Swami Ji** moved to the **Tikker Village, Kupwara** with some of his followers. There he established an **Ashram** on hill top.

Let me share a story which is quite famous amongst all the ardent devotees of **Swami Ji...**

In **Sharda**, Once a Sikh gentleman was being followed by some **Kabalis** who were interested in killing him. To save his life from those **Kabalis,** he ran away & was looking for a place to hide himself. At the end he found refuge in **Swami Ji's Ashram** in **Sharda.** Upon inquiry, the Sikh gentleman fearfully explained everything to **Swami Ji** & told him that he is going to get killed by those gunmen soon, he is going to die. He pleaded & begged **Swami Ji** for his life. While he was hiding in the Ashram, the gunmen were searching for him everywhere. The gunmen finally found him & asked him to face death. The Sikh started weeping loudly and begged for life from both. On this, **Swami Ji** consoled him and advised him not to worry but go down & see what they do.

The Sikh gentleman came down weeping to face the **Kabalis** and was asked to stand near the tree to face the bullets. Something unexpected happened !

The only available photograph of a Goddess Sharada Devi temple (Sharada Peeth) from Pakistan Occupied Kashmir (POK) before its destruction. A Kashmiri Pandit stands at the entrance, taken in 1893.

When they tried to press the trigger of their guns, the bullets failed to come out of their guns. They tried hard but nothing really happened. After trying thrice, the **Kabalis** bowed at the feet of **Swami Ji** and asked for his mercy. And that's how the Sikh gentleman was saved from **Kabalis**. The Kabalis then requested **Swami Ji** to leave that place as soon as possible since that was not a safe place to live. Post that incident,**Swami Ji** left for **Tikkar, Kupwara**.

SIX

MATA KHEER BHAWANI TIKKAR & SWAMI JI

Mata Kheer Bhawani Tikkar, Kupwara

Mata Kheer Bhawani Temple, Tikkar is dedicated to **MataRagnya Devi** who is an incarnation of **Goddess Durga**. This temple is constructed over a sacred spring popularly known as "**Amrit Kund**". It is believed that this sacred **Kund** has got some cosmic powers. It is also believed that this auspicious **Kund** is a form of **Mata Ragnya**. This holy spring (**Kund**) is known for changing its colour to different shades of red, pink, orange, green, blue, white etc. It is said that every colour indicates something. Like a

black shade is believed to be **inauspicious, unlucky**.

The Sacred Spring (Nag) of Mata Kheer Bhawani Temple, Tikkar

The term **Kheer** refers to the rice pudding that is offered to the sacred spring to impress the **Goddess**. The worship of **Kheer Bhawani** is universal among the **Hindus of Kashmir** & most of them worship her religously as their **Kuladevi or Ist devi**. The pandits of **Tikkar** village are ardent devotees of **Maa Ragnya** & they still visit the temple every year, coming from all parts of the world to seek blessings of **Mata**. Every year on **Zestha Asthami Mela**, thousands of pilgrims from all walks of life come to **Tikkar, Kupwara** and offer prayers to get their wishes fulfilled by **Mata Ragnya Bagwati**.

It is believed that **Goddess Ragnya** still lives here. Lots of saints & highly enlightened souls still visit this temple to seek blessings of **Mata Ragnya.** This place has got a lot of spritual significance amongst all the yogis & mahatmans. Every year, a big auspicious mela is organised here by **Mata Kheer Bhawani Asthapan Tikkar Kupwara** & is popular by the name "**Kheer Bhawani Mela**". It is one of the largest gatherings of Hindus in **Tikkar** region.

Mata is worshiped by many names including **Maharagnya Devi, Ragnya Devi, Rajni, Ragnya Bhagwati.**

Temple's Entrance

Tikkar village was used as a base Camp by **Sharda pilgrims** who used to visit **Sharda Temple** which is now in **Muzaffarabad** in **POK.** Swami Ji also was a great devotee of **Mata Ragnya** & had a lot of faith in her. When **Swami Ji** moved to **Tikkar,** he started living in the vicinity of the temple & sacred spring. He used to practice his sadhana over there.

It is said that on repeated requests of his devotees, **Swami Ji** thought of establishing an ashram in the vicinity of the temple. And when the devotees asked **Swami Ji**, which site should be used for building the Ashram ! **Swami Ji** took them to a site near the temple & asked them to start digging there.

<u>Swami Ji's Saligramwhich was found while digging</u> (*From his previous birth*)

Devotees started digging. In the middle of digging, **Swami Ji** cautioned his devotees not to get scared, if they see any snake or other deadly creature coming out, they wont cause any harm to them. After listening to **Swami Ji's** words, many of his devotees got frightened. As per **Swami Ji, big snakes** and **reptiles** did appear during the construction work but they quickly left the place without causing any harm to the devotees.

When devotees digged a few feet more, they were stunned to find a pair of **Tongs, a Kangri, a Chillum** and **some rice** under the earth. Along with all this, they also found a **Kangri**, a **Dhooni** with **Ash, one Saligram**

(Shivalinga) and some **fresh flowers**. All of them were surprised & perplexed. While seeing all this, one of his devotees, **Pt. Niranjan Nath**, who was lame by one leg, looked at **Swami Ji** in absolute astonishment.

At this, **Swami Ji** said these lines to him:

"Nera Langyo, kya vanay hal yath jayi kotah chhu mal"

English Translation: (How do I tell you, **Nera Lungu**, the secrets of this place, how many riches are hidden here).

After a further more digging, **Swami Ji** asked them to stop & not go beyond that... He told them that *"they are not yet prepared to see what's hidden there "*... Devotees were very much convinced that the site chosen by **Swami Ji** was not a normal site. It appeared to be the place where **Swami Ji** performed **Sadhana** in his previous **birth, janama.**

<u>Swami Ji's Cooking Place (Dhaan)</u>

As directed by the **Guru**, the devotees stopped digging further...**Swami Ji** instructed his devotees to take out the found articles and start raising the plinth with bricks and stones. Some of these articles are kept safely in the temple complex, untill now.

Swami Ji's Favourite Place, Tikkar

Swami Ji had a favourite place in the temple complex from where he used to sit & enjoy the view of many nearby areas. Also once, **Swami Ji** told one of his devotees that when he will leave his body, he would come from heaven to see this place. This place has become sacred to many of his devotees.

<u>Swami Nand Lal Ji's Kutiya (Tikkar, Kupwara)</u>

Swami Ji used to perform his sadhana & all yogic practices in his kutiya. This kutiya has no door, just a window to enter. **Swami Ji** used to meditate in this kutiya for hours. This kutiya is very dark from the inside which makes it a good place to meditate & do yog sadhana. One of **Swami Ji's** devotee has seen him meditating many feets up from the ground level. It is said that he used to bring his intestines out from his mouth through yogic practices, clean them & put them back inside.... That's so cool, right !

Swami Ji's Bed & Resting Chair

Whenever **Swami Ji** used to feel tired, he used to sit & relax in a room which is just above **Swami Ji's Kutiya.** It has a bed & a resting chair in it. Its still accessible to alldevotees. If you visit that place for darshan, you will also find **Swami Ji's** real **Khadav (Sandal)** there. The best part is that a devotee is allowed to sit & meditate there if he or she wants. This place has got a very different vibe, its so positive & calm. Any soul on this planet can find peace here.

<u>Swami Ji's Khadav</u> (Sandals)

If you have visited **Mata Kheer Bhawani Temple Tikkar**, you must be aware of the place known as **"Nav Chinaar"** or **"Nine Chinaar"**. If not then do visit this sacred place next time you visit **Mata Kheer Bhawani Temple, Tikkar. Swami Ji** himself planted the seeds of these nine chinaar trees. He called them "**Nine forms of Goddess Durga".** The interesting part is that these trees are still fresh & growing. **Swami Ji** used to meditate under these trees & called them of higher power. Devotees come here every year from different parts of the world & seek blessings of **Nav Durga.**

Nine Chinars, Nav Durga (Tikkar)

Saligram Temple, Tikkar

Under **Swami Ji's** supervision, a langar was held in the temple complex near **Swami Ji's Kutiya**. This **Langar** used to operate **24 hours a day, seven days a week** for the visitors! And **Swami Ji** used to make sure that no visitor leaves the temple complex without eating. **Swami Ji** would normally ask his devotees and sevaks in the **Ashram** to prepare more food as some devotees were on the way to see him, be it lunch time or dinner time. People have normally seen more than **15 to 20 persons** daily having food in his **Ashram** both in the morning and evening. He would never accept a penny from anybody. He avoided exposure and never used his unlimited powers to impress others. **Swami Ji's** life was very clean & simple like the nature he loved.

<u>Mata Kheer Bhawani Temple, Tikkar</u> (Aerial View)

Swami Ji did most of his sadhana in **Tikkar** village. **Tikkar Ashram** was inaugurated with great fanfare. **Swami Ji** loved to perform his routine **Sadhna** in the hilltop temple. The rush of devotees in **Tikkar Ashram** was significantly much more than other places. Very influential people of that area and far away areas were regular visitors of this Ashram.He used to spend his timethere performing religious & spiritual work for the betterment of mankind & society.

Currently, all activities of the temple are organised & managed by **Mata Kheer Bhawani Asthapan Commitee, Tikkar Kupwara.** Members of the commitee who themselves are ardent devotees of **Maa Ragnya** & **Swami Ji** are passionately trying to make experiance of the temple moreprofound and enriching. The commitee is proactively taking initiatives for the upgradation of the temple.

Pt. Raj Kishore is the priest of the temple who conducts all the daily prayers and performs all the rituals and ceremonies in the temple. He stays in the temple **24 hous a day, 365 days a year** & never misses a single prayer.

Mata Kheer Bhawani Temple, Tikkar has been shielded with multi-layered security to ensure high-level safety of the premises and yatris. **Commandos** trained in highly specialised **anti-terror tactics**, have been deployed at key vantage positions in and around the temple complex to make sure yatris have a **safe &divine darshan.** And that is the reason, no single news of terror attack or army killing comes from this temple.

May **MaaRagnya Bhagwati** bless us with all the **happiness, peace, love & prosperity** in the world... !

SEVEN
AGYAAN GATEY

The rush of devotees went on increasing and **Swami Ji** used to listen to each of his devotee, very patiently. Devotees from far off places started coming to meet **Swami Ji** for darshan and asked for his blessings. **Pandit Shridhar Joo Dhar (Ex. Conservator of Forests)** who himself was a highly awakened saint, **Sh. Jagan Nath Sumbly(Ex. Deputy Commissioner)** and **Sh. Soom Nath Halwai** were also some of his ardent devotees.

Late Mahatma Vibhishan Ji also was a disciple of **Swami Ji** who after many years of **Service and Sadhna** was initiated by **Swami Ji** in the ascetic order. **Swami Ji** met **Vibhishan Ji** for the first time in his kutiya near **Gowri-Pora village**. Also, he was one of the most loved disciples of **Swami Ji**. **Vibhishan Ji** was originally from **Baramulla** and his name was given to him by **Swami Ji** himself.

Swami Nand Lal Ji Maharaj

Swami Ji had a very strong & diverse personality. He acquired deep knowledge of **Ayurveda** and various other medicinal herbs. He also had an understanding of how **Ayurveda** can be used in treating different ailments. By using this skill, **Swami Ji** saved many people from some dangerous diseases. Miracles started happening.

Also, **Swami Ji** was a big fan of **Kashmiri Sufiana Mausiqi**, theclassical music of **Kashmir** (which uses its own **Maqams** & is accompanied by the **Rubab**, the **Kashmiri saz**, the **Santoor**, the **Wasool** and the **Dokra**). Sometimes, **Swami Ji** also used to play some sweet sufi ragas on a string-instrument called **Madham** and used to put the whole **Mehfil** of devotees in a trance state for hours. It is important to mention here that **Swami Ji** was a strict disciplinarian and never allowed any kind of deviation from the moral and ethical standards.

Lot of noteworthy saints used to come to meet **Swami Ji. Shri Ved Lal Ji** of **Hanjivera, Pattan,** popularly known as **Sed-Bab** and an accomplished saint used to visit **Swami Ji** frequently and accompanied him to different places. It is not clear if they were his disciples but the relationship was definitely special as both of them were seen engaged in some serious discourses. **Shri Ved Lal Ji** was given the name **Sed-Mol** by **Swami Ji** only for his **simplicity, devotion and straightforwardness.** This name was borrowed from the Guru of **LalDed** who was also called **Sed-Mol.** It is important to mention here that a **poet saint** who is famous for his devotional poetry, **Pandit Neelkanth Ji** of **Dab-Wakoora** village was also a **devotee** of **Swami Ji.** This man was simply exceptional & had some extraordinary writing skills. It is said that he could sing, compose & create beautiful couplets and bhajans instantly without much effort in front of many. He was famous for his sharp wit and **Swami Ji** had great regard for him. Some say he was not just a devotee of **Swami Ji** but a disciple initiated by him. However, the fact remains that **Pandit Neelkanth Ji** was fervently devoted to **Swami Ji** and both enjoyed each other's company.

It was **Pandit Neelkanth Ji** only, who wrote the famous **Gur-Astuti** of **Swami Ji ---**

Agnya'ne Ghat'y Sir'ye Praka'sh Chu'kh Aase'wonuy
Gyan'e Praka'sh Chu'kh Aase'wonuy
Hee M'yane Sat'guru Ksh'ene Ksh'ene Ch'um Aa'sare Cho'nuy

Guru-Astuti was sung at the lotus feet of **Paramguru Yogishwar Swami Nandlal JI Maharaj** by **Saint Shri Neelkanth ji Sharma** athis home in

Ganderbal. Gur-Astuti has a lot of significance in the lives of Swami Ji's devotees. **Agyaan Gatey** is a powerful Bhajan in the lucid form of **Mantrik Bhajans** of **Kashmir Bhakti** tradition. This **Astuti** works like a sacred thread between **Swami Ji** & his devotees. Even today, **Swami Ji's** devotees sing this astuti as a prayer everyday with utmost devotion & love to seek **Swami Ji's** blessings. It is believed that this **astuti** was made in the presence of **Swami Ji** & is considered to be very powerful.

<u>**Pandit Neelkanth Ji**</u>

And yes, that reminds me of a very interesting story from the past which is also very popular among the devotees....

It is said that once upon a time when **Swami Nand Lal Ji** entered the **front yard (aangan)** of his dear diciple **Shri Neelkanth Ji**, hewent into the ecstasy mode of **Karuna Bhaava** & sat down somewhere in the aangan. After seeing his Guru in front of his eyes like that, **Nilkanth ji** then & there started reciting the **Guru-Astuti** to his **Guru, Yogiraj Swami Nand Lal Ji Maharaj.**

Some of us dont understand the real meaning of **Guru-Astuti** because of certain language barriers & difficulties. So, lets decode it & see what **Pandit**

Neelkanth Ji is trying to express through **"Agyaan Gatey"**...

Translation of Guru-Astuti, Agyaan Gatey with meaning in **English** :-

Agyaan Gatey Siri Prakash Chhukh Aaswunuyi

Gyaan Prakash Chhukh Aaswunuyi

Om Shri Sat Gvara Khana Khyena Chum Assara Chonuy

O my Sadguru---I rely on your compassion and grace in each and every moment of my life. You are the radiance of the Sun; enlightening me during my hours of ignorance. You are OM and you are Shri/the auspiciousness. You are the true guru/preceptor.

Tsuyi Chhuk Brahma Chuyi vishnu Maheshwarai

Chuyi Vishwamaya Chhuk Ajar Amar Akhshar Theyrai

Par Treyn Bhuwanan Paadi Pranaam Bawinay Myonuya

Shri Sat Gvara Khyen Khyen Chhum Asara Chonuyi

You are Brahma--the creator, Vishnu--the sustainer and Maheshwara--the great force of dissolution, or merger. You are Ajara/changeless, Absolute; immortal, infinite and immutable. I offer my laudations to you--as you are existing in the three worlds of "Bhu Bhuvah and Swah".

O my Sadguru---I rely on you in each and every moment of my life

Chaanyen Padan Hundi Garde Hunduya Anjan
yus Laagi nyetran Divya Drishti Tamis Chhi Banan
Yeth Nu Kaanh WuChaan Tath Sadaa Chhukh WuChwunuyi
Shri Satgura Khyen Khyen Chhum Asara Chonuyi

Any one can realize the supreme truth and attain the Divine vision, if there is complete surrender at your feet, by annointing his/her eyes with the dust of your lotus feet. That truth---higher realization not seen by others is always viewed by you. O my Sadguru---I rely on you in each and every moment of my life

Daya Sagar Kar Mey Daya Deenas Heenas
Siddhi Ditam Mad Mochan mye Buddhi Hiinas
Ba Ada kas wana Aaírit Naad Chhuk Bozwunuya
Shri Satgura Khyen Khyen Chhum Asara Chonuyi

Being a compassionate One, please grace me with the Siddhi/perfection. I am proud with ignorance about Truth. I am unaware of my intelligence without any intelligence, thus you can take the pride away from my being. I can not share my sadness with any one, except your noble self. Because you listen to my inner psyche. O my Sadguru---I rely on you in each and every moment of my life

Sharan Bu Aasay Tsey Pyosay Paran Paadan
Warum Mey Daasas Thawatam Kan Aaírtyen Naadan
Taran Bhawa sar Yimaw Chonuyi Prebhaav Zonuyi
Shri Satgura Khyen Khyen Chhum Asara Chonuyi

I have come and prostrate before you. Bless me with your grace, listen to my wooing sounds. They will attain liberation, who understand your spiritual aura filled with inner strength of Atman.
O my Sadguru---I rely on you in each and every moment of my life.

Chhuk Sidhi Yogi Bu Chhus Ruugi Tsu dim Dawa
Aushad Chaanyen Paadan Hunz Garda Chhana
Uttan Chuuran Sarva Roogan Chhuya Haa Kaaswun
Shri Satgura Khyen Khyen Chhum Asara Chonuyi

Beyond doubt, you are an embodiment of Sidha Yogi--a perfect Yogi--, but I am an ailing person, and need the spiritual help to get evolved, which would raise my spiritual bent of mind for higher understanding of the truth. O my Sadguru---I rely on you in each and every moment of my life.

Ghate Gaashar! Chaani dayaayi Mye Roog Hate
Mate Chhusaya Taar Bhava Sara Ake Wyote
Late Ake Mwakh Mye Haawtam Prazalwunuya
Shri Satgura Khyen Khyen Chhum Asara Chonuyi

You are the source of light in the spell of darkness. I am sure you will relieve me of the ailments caused by my ignorance. I am dependent on your grace for transcending myself from the ocean of Samsara, within a time span of single jump taking. Please be gracious enough to show the beautiful face, radiant with spirituality. O my Sadguru---I rely on you in each and every moment of my life.

Santap Agan Paapaw Suti Gomut Prabal
Sheras Pyeth Thav KarKamal Panun Shital
Santap tsalyem Paph Galyem Now tai Prionuyi
Shri Satgura Khyen Khyen Chhum Asara Chonuyi

I have become agitated with the sins associated with the wrong doings. Please place your cool palm on my head, so that the wrath of 'Tamas'--inertia will be transformed, for higher spiritual values.
O my Sadguru---I rely on you in each and every moment of my life.

Setar Manuk Taar Chaírith Sada Diwan
Had Yeth No kuney Bvadh myani soy tvata gewaan
Vrits myani natsan kanaw boztam Lol Wanawunuyi
Shri Satgura Khyen Khyen Chhum Asara Chonuyi

The Sitar of my mind is vibrating , when I tightened the cords. Now I sing the songs dedicated to your spiritual self. The emotive nature of psychic being is now dancing to the tune of non-dualistic melody.
O my Sadguru---I rely on you in each and every moment of my life

Kartam Sa Daya Vartam Tal Charnarbendan
Chhukh Bodh Drishti tsuyi Diwan anyen Tu myendyen
Andan Chhi nyaay Chaani Dayayi kar Paay Myonuyi
Shri Satgura Khyen Khyen Chhum Asara Chonuyi

Take mercy on me. Grant me refuge to have presence near your lotus feet. Your intuitive ability helps the blind to go ahead in action and a lepar to be full in spirits. You are just in nature and you deliver justice through your grace. O my Sadguru---I rely on you in each and every moment of my life.

Chintamano! Svan Tsu Banawan Chukh Tramas
Fotas Mokhtai Pvakhta Banawan Chukh Tramas
Tsu Gati Hund gaash Swami Nand Lal Chu Naw Chonuyi
Shri Satgura Khyen Khyen Chhum Asara Chonuyi

You are Chintamani--a touch stone to convert copper into gold. It is because of meditation that true Advaita/ non-dualism takes place between a disiple and a preceptor. The humility and humbleness in a Shishya makeshim/herb to ascend to the spiritual heights.
O my Sadguru---I rely on you in each and every moment of my life.

Yi Bu Nu oasus Tiiy Oasus Zaanaan Bu paanai
Dayayi Chanye Yi Bu Chhus Ti mye Zonum Paanai
Rowmut Lobum pazi Labith na Zi Raawrawun
Shri Satgura Khyen Khyen Chhum Asara Chonuyi

I was of the notion that I am only flesh and bone, the material self but was not aware of the true self--which is pure Atman abiding in my being. It is because of your grace that I could realize that I am pure Atman--Self. I got this identity, now I should preserve it to the best of my spiritual efforts and understanding. O my Sadguru---I rely on you in each and every moment of my life.

Timan zi Yiman Gaw Zi Yiman Tse Suti Layas
Dayas Suutyen gayi Zu Miilith Waitis Payas
Bhayas Zay Gokh Dwan haa Ruudukh Kunuy Baswunuyi
Shri Satgura Khyen Khyen Chhum Asara Chonuyi

Those who got merged in your spiritual self and became one with Atman...., they got absorbed in the spiritual realm of Divinity. The fear of being in this Samsara got vanished and they achieved their true self of being pure Atman. O my Sadguru---I rely on you in each and every moment of my life.

Bhava Sar Tarnuk Neel Kanthas Banitan Wyapaay
Swami NandLal Ji Tai Swami Lal; Ji Ruuzitan Sahaay

Chhi Tang Aamutyi Anzal Hyeth Chhi Mamgawunyi
Shri Satgura Khyen Khyen Chhum Asara Chonuyi

Neel Kanth makes a humble submission to receive the blessings in the spiritual manner as how could he cross the oceanic world of transmigration of soul. May Swami Nand Lal Ji and his Guru Swami Lal Ji be always graceful to him!

Really, we have been in great agony,pain and suffering. We ask for a boon of spiritual involution --a meaningful life force to sustain our selves. Be it so!

O my Sadguru---I rely on you in each and every moment of my life...

Shri Neelkanth ji's devotion to his Guru is further depicted in another popular bhajan popularly known as *"Shiv Leela"* and one can feel his devotion by reading the last couplet of the Leela...

Sh.Neelkanths Sant Nandlal ji yan vanuyi
Vanu Shiv Sundhyu Ghokals Andar yinuyi
Shanker tu Krishan--Krishan Tu Shanker chuy no beyunuyi

Who was **Pandit Neelkanth Ji** & why he was so dear to **Swami Ji** ?

Pt. Neelkanth Ji Sharma, a saint and poet of highest order possessed miraculous characteristics and an attractive personality. Born in a middle class **Kashmiri Pandit family** of **Atri Bhargave Gotra**, in **1888 AD** was the most loved child of his parents. The family had a rich spiritual, religious and literally background. Pt. **Neelkhant ji's** father **Pt. Shankar Nath Ji Sharma** and mother **Smt. Sukhmali Devi** were devotes of **Shri Rama Pandit ji. In** this way **Neelkanth Ji** inherited **Ramabhakti** and spirituality from his parents.

Pandit Neelkanth Ji

Pt. Shankarnath ji arranged teachers to teach sanskrit language to his beloved son at home. After learning some basics of the language **Neelkanth ji** with his own gifted intelligence and urge mastered the language. He not only mastered the language but also achieved great depth in **Vedanta and Shaiva Philosophies.** Besides that he also mastered some other languages like **Persian, Urdu and Hindi** on his own. Apart from that he also studied **shastras** thoroughly including **Jyotish shastra.** He was an authority on **phalit jyotish.** His forecasts & predictions were true always. It is also said that he had attained **vakhsidhi.** Although, he never went to any school or college but many scholars used to come to him to clear their doubts. He was never seen angry with anybody, not even his children or other family members.

Pt. Neelkanth ji started doing his sadhana since his early boyhood. He strongly believed that God is one and is worshiped by countless names. **Pandit ji** used to do pooja of a clay-made shivalinga daily for **three to four hours.Panditji** composed **250 to 300 poems (Leelas)** in **Kashmiri** in praise of **Rama, Krishna, Shiva and Matabhavani.** He also authored **SHARMA RAMAYANA (KASHMIRI RAMAYAN),BHAKHTA JAIDEV CHRITA** and a drama named **BILWA MANGAL NATAK.Pandit ji** was a very good translator as well. He translated **Bhagwat Geeta** in **Kashmiri language** and named it as **SUDHA SINDHU.** One of Bhasa's masterpiece **SWAPNA VASAWADATTAM** was also translated by him into beautiful **Kashmiri prose and poetry.** He was of the opinion that composing and singing of leelas is a form of **sadhana.**

There's another remarkable poem which came into existence due to the celestial union of **Swami Ji** & **Pandit Neelkanth Ji.** This poem depicts a very beautiful incident from the past, when **Lord Shiva** in the form of a Sanyasi visits **Maa Yashodha's** house in **Gokul** just to have a glimpse of **Little Krishna.** The poem was recited by **Pandit Neelkanth Ji** in the presence of **Swami Ji** on his holy desire, probably in **Swami Ji's Kutiya.** And interestingly this fact is rendered very beautifully in last stanza of this poem---

Yee Neel Kanthas Sant Nand Lal Jeean Wonuy
Wan Shive Sunduy Gokulas Undher Yunuy
Shankar Te Krishen, Krishene Shankar Chuy No Byunuy
Shod Bodh Shankar Aav Laaran Gokul Kuny
Azar Amar Yugheshur Nirmal Kunuy

EIGHT
MIRACLES OF SWAMI NAND LAL JI

While it is difficult to recall all the miracles attributed to **Swami Ji** but an effort can be made to mention some of them here....

So, lets start!

Once upon a time, in **Sopore**, around **1960-61**, when **Swami Ji** was living in a temple, a poojari came to him screaming loud that his wife has died. **Swami Ji** took pity on him and told him not to shout loud but go to the nearby river **Vitasta** and bring a small tumbler, full of water. When he came back, he was told to sprinkle some water from that tumbler on the face of his wife. When he followed **Swami Ji's** direction, he found that after a few minutes, his wife came back to life and is said to have lived longer than her husband.

<u>Swami Nand Lal Ji Maharaj</u>

On another occasion, one of **Swami Ji's** ardent disciples passed away. While his body was being bathed, he suddenly woke up to the chagrin of people around him. People got frightened to see the dead person coming back to life. The dead devotee, back in life, told them "**please, don't be afraid of me, give me some clothes to wear, I will narrate to you the reason of my revival**" which he later on did. But since such revelation was not ordered by **Swami Ji**, the devotee lost his power of speech even though he survived for a long time. This miracle happened after **Swami Ji** had attained **Nirvana**.

Once before leaving for **Delhi, Swami Ji** stayed at **Jawahar Nagar** in the house of a devotee. When the 15-year old son of the devotee bowed before **Swami Ji** as usual in the morning, a thought flashed across his and that the photograph of **Lord Shiva** adorning the wall was just a fiction. **Swami Ji** understood the boy's inner thoughts and threw an innocent smile. During the night, when the boy went to bed in his room, where his cousin also slept, at dead of the night he suddenly opened his eyes on seeing flashes of light having engulfed the room. Unable to stand the glare, he tried to cover his eyes and head with bed sheets, but the glare flashed even through the sheets. Ultimately, he got up and to his surprise, found **Lord Shiva** sitting and smiling on a chair with trillions of lights surrounding him. After some time, everything came back to normal. In the morning, he went again to **Swami Ji** as usual and paid his obeisance at his feet; **Swami Ji** smiled and asked him whether there was any sense in **Lord Shiva's** photograph now. The boy prostrated before **Swami Ji** and begged for his mercy.

There's one more incident about a devotee of **Swami Ji** who was working in the **Revenue Department** at **Handwara/Sopore**. As a consequence of some of his **misdeeds** and **misappropriations**, he was to be sentenced by the court. A day before the judgement, he came to **Swami Ji's Ashram** and begged for mercy. While listening to him, **Swami Ji** took a long puff from his chillum & a big flash of fire appeared. **Swami Ji** told him to calm down and forget his worry. To the devotee's luck, the concerned court premises were suddenly engulfed by a ravaging fire, with the entire building and court records being reduced to ashes, thus giving him a reprieve for life.

<u>Swami Nand Lal Ji Maharaj</u>

It reminds me of one more story...

A retired pandit police officer used to visit **Swami Ji's Ashram** in **Tikkar** occasionally. One day, he had fallen sick & suddenly had to rush to **SMHS Hospital in Srinagar** with his wife & some relatives. He was in a very serious condition. That night, the patient's condition got worse & he died all of a sudden. Seeing this, his wife starting crying and screaming out loud. And after final confirmation of patient's death, doctors started shifting the dead body like with any other dead body. After a couple of hours...

The patient's wife, who was sitting just next to the **dead body** was **frightened** when she saw the **dead body** moving & coming back to life. She thought, some **evil spirit** had overtaken her husband's body. She was **awestruck & amazed** by all what was happening. She curiously observed the movements of her husband from a far off distance who was waving his hand & was calling her. She refused to go near him.

A relative arrived early in the morning with some medicines & got to know everything what all happened last night. The wife was so scared, she even stopped her relative to go near the dead person. Mustering courage, he did go near the body and the person who was back to life, requested his relative to take him back to his home. He said "**I have been granted new life and shall narrate to you all the details at home**".

On reaching home, the revived person asked his relative to pull out a thorn from his foot. It was removed instantaneously and was found to be actually a nail. The person was thus relieved of acute pain and agony caused by the **nail-like thorn**. The person started sharing his surreal experiance. He said "Two people came & picked me up from the **Hospital**. They took me to a hall which resembled a **cinema theatre**. And there I saw the entire doings of my life recorded and played before me just like a film, which also featured my presence in **Swami Ji's Ashram**.

Swami Nand Lal Ji's Ashram & Kutiya (Tikkar, Kupwara)

Inside Swami Ji's Ashram(Tikkar, Kupwara)

After watching the whole thing, I was taken to a **hill-top**. From the **hill-top**, I was made to see two magical spaces: On one side, there were **beautifulrich gardens** and on the other side, a **dense black forest.** One of the escorts pushed me towards the **black forest** where at a distance I saw **Swami Ji** sitting & puffing his **chillum.** Suddenly a thorn stuck to my foot causing severe pain. After a while, **Swami Ji** directed the escorts to take me back. And that's how I came back to life".

The thorn, which looked like an iron nail, was preserved by the police officer till his death.

<u>The Miraculous Story of Three Old Pandits - Bhrama, Vishnu & Maheshwar</u>

One day, one of **Swami Ji's** disciples, **Jai Kishan** (By Name) started thinking of **Brahma, Vishnu and Maheshwar** and was curious to know who they really were. In the evening when sun had set and the moon was at its zenith, he heard **Swami Ji** directing **Vibhishan Ji** to bring some tea for the guests who were sitting with him.

So, **Vibhishan Ji** brought a **Samawar** full of tea & **Jai Kishan** was accompanying him with some **Khosoos(Cups). Three Old Pandits, 80 to 90 years** of age with white beards and wearing R**ound Kashmiri Turbans** with

long-armed pherans were seen chatting with **Swami Ji**. When the guests were leaving, **Swami Ji** directed **Jai Kishan** to accompany them upto the main road which was half a mile or so from the **Ashram**. In deference to **Swami Ji's** orders, **Jai Kishan** accompanied the **Three Old Pandits** to the Road. When he reached the gate of the **Ashram**, he heard **Swami Ji** calling him. He just looked back for a second to verify whether he was actually being called. But when he regained his posture, to his surprise he found all the three **Pandits** missing. He got worried & ran from here and there for an hour in all directions in search of them. During the night, he came back to **Swami Ji** (his Guru).**Jaikishan** was confused when he saw **Swami Ji** smiling like a kid. On this, **Swami Ji** told him, "Don't worry, this is an answer to the question that arosed in your mind this morning. The **Three Pandits** you are searching for since morning were actually the "**Trikoti - Brahma, Vishnu and Maheshwar**".

Brahma, Vishnu & Maheshwar

One day, **Swami Ji** asked **Jai Kishan** if he would like to go on a **World Tour**. **Jai Kishen** was confused & remained quite. After a while, **Swami Ji** told him to make all the preparations. Unexpectedly soon, he was informed by his seniors at work that he has been transferred to the security wing of **Prime Minister's Office. P.M.Mrs. Indra Ghandhi** had to travel to some countries by **INS Vikrant (An Aircraft Carrier in Service with Indian Navy;**

Year 1961)& **Jai Kishan** was in the security wing of the **Prime Minister**. And that became the reason for his world tour that too with **Mrs. Indra Gandhi**.

In early **1967**, **Swami Ji** already had prophesied that **Kashmiri Pandits** will be in big trouble, soon. **Swami Ji** ordained that a big sacrifice will be required to save the community.

In **Boomai**, where **Swami Ji** stayed for some time, a Muslim by the name of **Mohammed Gosain**, one day saw **Swami Ji** sitting in naked form with **Trishul** in hand travelling on **Nandi**. He then & there became a ardent devotee of **Swami Ji**.

Swami Ji's Statue

Another Muslim came to **Swami Ji** and told him that his cow is not giving milk any more. **Swami Ji** directed him to go to his cow and tell her to give some milk for **Nand Lal**. He followed **Swami Ji's** directions and uttered the same lines before the cow and the cow instantly started giving milk.

There is yet another interesting incident. In **Hoshura**, a young Pandit boy always had a wish to work as a volunteer in **Congo, Africa**. **Swami Ji** asked him, "**Congo alone! Why not a World Tour?**" And after some days, this boy was given a job of driver in the **CongoArmy** by the **Govt. of Congo**. And his office in **Congo** was located near the **Airport** where many airplanes used to take off and land.

So, one day when he was given the job of supervising cargo loading, he mistakenly boarded a plane which was heading to **Washington**. And he himself was not aware of the fact that he was on a journey of world tour which **Swami Ji** had planned for him. This flight's first destination was **Washington**, followed by many other cities and its return was after one month.

This gentleman, after coming from this unplanned unpaid world tour came back to **India** and was serving as a **Postmaster** when people last saw him.

In **October 1947** when tribal raiders invaded and entered **Kashmir.** They started massive killing and looting **Non-Muslims** areas. **Swami Ji** started marching towards **Bomai** village with some of his devotees. When **Swami Ji** entered **Bomai**, he saw that **Pandits ofBomai** were scared beyond measure and were preparing for every eventuality. **Swami Ji** instructed them to be contented and be at their places. And then a miracle happened....

None of the millitants entered **Bomai** though the **Pandits** in that village were good in number and all prosperous. It is said that some kind of confusion occured between those millitants and they didn't venture entering **Bomai,** till they were hounded back by **Indian Army**.

Swami Ji's miracles continue to take place even after his **Nirvana** insofar as his devotees are concerned. He is omnipresent and always available to guide his ardent seekers.

NINE

THE PERFECT MASTER

Swami Nand Lal Ji Maharaj

Swami Ji was a perfect master & used to do his **YogaSadhana** on a routine basis. His **YogicSadhana** included **various postures** and **Pranayama.** He also used to do**Dhoti-Kriya** for purification. **Swami Ji** used to stay absorbed in deep studies & readings of various scriptures. He was habitual of smoking **Charas and Tobacco**. Otherwise he maintained very clean habits and his **Kutiya** always exhibited a flavour of calmness and purity. Though many of his devotees used to be with him & were ready to do all kinds of jobs for him but he personally used to look after the Cleanliness of his **Kutiya & Ashram**. During summers, **Swami Ji** sometimes used to lay his **Aasana** or sit on an elevated space outside the **Ashram** & the devotees used to sit in front of him and listen to his **discourses/lectures** carefully. All the visitorswere welcomed by him warmly and were always served with a cup of "**Kehva**, a **Traditional Kashmiri Tea**". **Swami Ji** also used to take a few sips of the **Kehva** but after having some, he used to offer it to some of his devotees as a **Prasad**. The evenings with **Swami Ji** were quite attractive, people used to sing/recite **Bhajans/Leelas** & **Swami Ji** also used to participate in that session. When it comes to food, **Swami Ji** was a strict vegetarian & he stayed like that all his life. He used to eat very simple **Satvik** food and avoided onions, garlic, tomatoes and some leafy vegetables. His preferred list of food included **Plain Rice, Kashmiri Saag, Moong Dal** and **Nadru (Lotus Stem)**. **Swami Ji** used to observe fast on many days especially **Ashtami, Puranmashi, Amavasya, Ekadashi and other auspicious days**. **Swami Ji** himself used to prepare many kinds of **pickles and medicinal preparations** in small glass bottles. He used to keep them outside his **Kutiya** on the **verandah** in open sun and he probably used them in curing patients who came to him.

TEN
MAHASAMADHI

His Holiness, **Swami Ji** attained **Nirvana** or went into **Mahasamadhi** in **Malviya Nagar, Delhi** in the year **1966.** It was **January**, on the day of **Gauri Triteya**, in the house of **Pandit Prem Nath Sadhu (Swami Ji's Devotee),** he attained **Eternal Samadhi.**

<u>Funeral of Swami Nand Lal Ji Maharaj (Shouldered by Swami Sed Bab Ji, Swami Mast Bab Ji, Swami Vibhishan Ji & some other dignitaries)</u>

Swami Ji left us way too soon but he will stay in our hearts, forever. He left behind some interesting stories to talk about. **Swami Ji** was a saint with a mission. A mission of opening the door of spirituality in people's lives & evolving them to the state of godliness. He left no stone unturned to fulfill his mission and succeeded in transforming thousands of lives around him. Even after **Swami Ji's** celestial flight **(Mahasamadhi)**, the love of his devotees towards him stayed unchanged. In today's times, **Swami Ji** is worshiped & followed by thousands of **Hindus** in **India & Outside**. For a devotee, **Swami Ji** means everything !..... & This fact is appropriately described in the these lines from the famous **Guru-Astuti** penned by **Late Shri Neelkanth Ji** :

O My Satguru! I Depend Only Upon Your Moral Support Every Moment
In The Darkness Of My Ignorance You Are Always A Beacon Light Like Sun
To Show Me Way Out From Darkness To Light.....
--------------Jai Guru Maharaj--------------

Author's Bio

Aneesh Trakroo is a celebrated critically acclaimed **author, poet & content writer** from **Tikkar** villageof **Kupwara District, Kashmir**. Grandson of the poet-saint **Pandit Poshkar Nath Trakroo,** he is a die-hard devotee of "**Swami Nand Lal Ji Maharaj**". His debut novel **"52 Days of Wanderlust"** was published by **Notion Press Publications** in the year **2019** & after the success of his first book, within a year he published two more books. **Aneesh Trakroo** is a true creative at heart, with a passion for **music, theatre and writing**. His artistic endeavors serve as a means of self-expression and allow him to explore the world through different mediums. Aneesh's work often captures the beauty of everyday life, showcasing the extraordinary in the ordinary.